The Biography of Magnus Carlsen

The Biog\
Magnus C\

How a Modern Master Changed the Face
of Chess

Ben Gold

The Biography of Magnus Carlsen

Copyright By The Author
All Rights Reserved

The Biography of Magnus Carlsen

TABLE OF CONTENTS

INTRODUCTION 5

Chapter 1: Childhood and Family History 10

    Norwegian Childhood 10

    Support and Influence from Families 15

    Early Talent Indications 20

    Initial Experiences with Chess 24

Chapter 2: Ascent in the World of Chess 31

    Young Contests and Early Victories 31

    Instruction and Guidance 35

    Groundbreaking Acts 41

    Acknowledgment on the International Scene 46

Chapter 3: Taking on the Role of Grandmaster 51

    The Path to the General Manager Title 51

    Important Matches and Rivals 56

    Playing Style and Strategies 61

    Overcoming Obstacles 67

Chapter 4: Champion of World Chess 73

    The Championship Journey 73

    Overcoming Anand Viswanathan 78

    Rivalries and Title Defenses 85

    Effect on the Community of Chess Players 92

Chapter 5: Beyond Chess, Life 99

    Hobbies and Interests..100
    Media Presences and Support 107
    Entrepreneurship..115
    Contribution to the Popularization of Chess.....123

Chapter 6: History and Prospects...........................131
    Inputs into the Game 132
    The Inspirational and Mentoring Role 139
    Accomplishments and Honors 146
    Looking Ahead 154

The Biography of Magnus Carlsen

INTRODUCTION

The name Magnus Carlsen has resonance that extends well beyond the sixty-four squares of a chessboard. Often referred to as the "Mozart of Chess," he has revolutionized the modern grandmaster's role. In addition to talent and hard effort, his journey from a modest Norwegian youngster to the top of the chess world is a narrative of unrelenting curiosity, fearless competition, and an unflinching belief in one's own ability. The astonishing journey of this extraordinary mind, whose accomplishments have enthralled millions and motivated a new generation of chess aficionados, is examined in The Biography of Magnus Carlsen.

Sven Magnus Øen Carlsen was born in 1990 in Tønsberg, Norway, and showed remarkable intelligence at a young age. He

The Biography of Magnus Carlsen

was a kid who loved puzzles, numbers, and patterns long before his name was associated with world titles and ratings that broke records. His early years were characterized by an exceptional capacity for memory recall and problem-solving, abilities that would soon be best utilized in the game of chess.

In addition to his extraordinary talent, Carlsen's story is captivating because of the way he has combined traditional craftsmanship with contemporary energy. He is a player who loves originality and surprise while yet honoring the traditional chess traditions. He frequently takes games into uncharted areas where his opponents are least at ease. He has defeated the finest players in the world thanks to his special combination of preparation and spontaneity,

The Biography of Magnus Carlsen

solidifying his status as one of the greatest players in history.

Carlsen has continuously pushed the envelope over his career. He was already gaining notoriety at the age of 13 for taking on seasoned grandmasters without fear. He became the youngest player in history to reach the top of the FIDE world rankings at the age of 19. He defeated the renowned Viswanathan Anand in 2013 to win the title of World Chess Champion, ushering in an era characterized by his competitive tenacity and perceptive technique. His reputation as a contemporary chess legend has only grown stronger as a result of his consecutive title defenses.

Magnus Carlsen's influence, however, extends much beyond the chessboard. He has embraced technology and media, interacting with fans all around the world through channels like mobile chess apps and internet broadcasting. His contributions to initiatives like the Champions Chess Tour and Play Magnus have elevated the game to previously unheard-of levels of excitement and accessibility. By doing this, he has been instrumental in turning chess from a specialized cerebral activity into a popular sport around the world.

The goal of this biography is to look beyond the numbers, wins, and accolades. It seeks to expose the grandmaster's inner self, including his periods of uncertainty, inspiration, the impact of mentors and family, and his unwavering desire to better himself. The biography of Magnus Carlsen offers important lessons on brilliance, tenacity, and enthusiasm, regardless of whether you are a

The Biography of Magnus Carlsen

lifetime chess enthusiast or a novice attracted by the recent worldwide chess boom.

Chapter 1: Childhood and Family History

Norwegian Childhood

Magnus Carlsen was born Sven Magnus Øen Carlsen in Tønsberg, Norway, on November 30, 1990. His birth occurred amid a time of silent change in his native nation. In the early 1990s, Norway was renowned for its unspoiled landscapes, robust welfare system, and a national identity influenced by both communal collaboration and tough independence. Tønsberg, the town where Magnus was born, is historically significant because it is thought to be the oldest in Norway and has Viking roots. His early years were surrounded by its picturesque harbors, medieval ruins, and mild coastal air.

The Biography of Magnus Carlsen

Magnus joined his older sister Ellen as the second child of Henrik Albert Carlsen and Sigrun Øen. Two additional girls, Ingrid and Signe, would later join the Carlsen family, forming a cozy home with the energy, conversation, and sometimes mayhem of a vibrant sibling group. Magnus was characterized from the start by qualities uncommon for a boy of his age, including silent observation, intense focus, and an eerie memory, according to those close to the family.

A Pattern-Driven Mind

Magnus had a natural interest in riddles, patterns, and construction long before chess ever came into his life. By the time he was two years old, his parents remember, he was able to put together intricate jigsaw puzzles meant for kids twice his age. He wasn't only piecing things together mechanically; instead, he had a clear strategy and was moving toward the finished vision in his mind. Similarly, Magnus's ability to recognize the flags of almost every nation in the globe by the age of five perplexed his family friends. He would eventually use this visual-spatial intelligence as the basis for his chess skills.

Norwegian Countryside Life

The family relocated to Lommedalen, a tiny valley town about 20 kilometers from Oslo that is encircled by hills and forests, when Magnus was still very young. Much of his early life would be influenced by this move. Lommedalen provided a harmony between intimate community and peaceful seclusion. The valley was turned into a playground by the snow throughout the winter, with skiing, sledding, and snowball battles offering nonstop fun. Hikes, bike rides, and outdoor play extended well into the evening during the summer's long daylight hours.

Magnus found that these natural settings fostered both his physical vitality and his capacity for sustained concentration. Only the regularity of the seasons and the support of a family that valued education were present, rather than the cacophonous distractions of city life.

Social Life and School Days

Magnus had a combination of intelligence and introversion during his early school years. Instructors soon discovered that he was capable of learning far more than was taught in the classroom. Magnus was already solving challenging puzzles, learning entire volumes of information by heart, and

The Biography of Magnus Carlsen

exhibiting abilities that set him apart from his contemporaries, who were only learning the fundamentals of addition and subtraction. However, he wasn't always keen to show off his skills in public. In the classroom, he tended to participate quietly rather than compete loudly. His strongest ties were to his family, particularly his sisters, with whom he spent endless hours playing, telling stories, and playing games.

Magnus fit in well with Norway's school system, which places a significant emphasis on personal development and curiosity. While still taking part in group activities, his teachers let him work alone on difficult topics. For a boy whose gifts could have normally caused him to feel isolated, these early liberties provided him with the confidence to pursue his intellectual pursuits without worrying about being mocked.

Support and Influence from Families

Magnus's family provided the oxygen necessary for his skill to develop into a stable flame, if it were a spark. Although Henrik and Sigrun were steadfast in their efforts to provide a loving home for each of their children, they soon realized that Magnus's requirements were a little different.

Parents as Mentors, Not Autocrats

Despite not being a professional chess player, Henrik was an engineer by training with a sharp analytical mind who was captivated by strategy and problem-solving. Chemical engineer Sigrun struck a balance between her scientific expertise and compassion. Together, they provided their home with both

The Biography of Magnus Carlsen

emotional stability and intellectual stimulation. They were never the type of parents who made their kids participate in particular activities against their will. Rather, they exposed children to a variety of activities, such as games, athletics, reading, and art, and they saw where each child's interests naturally led.

That fascination quickly shifted to chess for Magnus. When he was five years old, his father started him playing the game as a family pastime rather than as a structured lesson. Magnus initially showed a moderate level of interest, favoring outside games and Lego structures. But after a while of observing, he realized that chess provided the same strategic thinking, spatial reasoning, and pattern recognition that he already enjoyed.

A Family that Placed a High Value on Education

Books filled the shelves of the Carlsen residence, and discussions frequently veered toward subjects like history, physics, and current affairs. The purpose of dinnertime was to discuss ideas, debate viewpoints, and, sometimes, make fun of one another through trivia competitions. This ongoing mental activity was just a part of the family's lifestyle and wasn't intended to promote academic success for its own sake.

Magnus's sisters were also very important. The oldest, Ellen, was a friend and a game-rival. Whether playing sports, board games, or chess, their matches were always cordial despite their intense rivalry. Magnus's life never became just about intellectual pursuits thanks to the fun and feeling of balance that the younger sisters, Ingrid and Signe, provided. They helped him stay grounded by reminding him that his family came before his own goals.

Promoting Self-Sufficiency and Travel

The Carlsens' frequent weeks-long or months-long family vacations were one of their most important choices. These trips were immersive experiences that introduced the kids to various cultures, languages, and historical periods rather than opulent getaways. Magnus took in everything he encountered, whether it was strolling through the streets of Paris, touring Eastern European castles, or trekking across the Alps. In addition to expanding his horizons, travel helped him develop the flexibility and fortitude that would eventually enable him to handle the demands of competing internationally in chess.

Support and Freedom in Balance

Henrik and Sigrun were unique among prodigy parents in that they refused to overly control their son's growth. While providing direction, materials, and emotional support, they let Magnus go at his own speed. They urged him to spend hours playing chess. It was also acceptable for him to take a break and spend an afternoon building Lego structures. His love for chess was able to develop organically because of this harmony between structure and freedom, which guards against burnout, a common problem for gifted young players.

Early Talent Indications

Magnus Carlsen showed aptitudes that were hard to ignore from a young age. Magnus appeared to have an exceptionally wide range of cognitive abilities, including logical reasoning, visual-spatial intelligence, intense attention, and an exceptional memory, whereas some kids only exhibit precocity in a limited domain.

The Master of Puzzles

Magnus's main passion was puzzles, including jigsaws, crosswords, mazes, and three-dimensional construction sets, before chess became a significant part of his life. By the age of two, he was already putting together puzzles meant for much older kids, demonstrating not only perseverance through trial and error but also the capacity to see the finished product beforehand. Later, his father Henrik described seeing him solve a 50-piece puzzle with the composed concentration of an adult, rotating each piece in his tiny hands until it fit together purposefully.

His desire for complexity only deepened as he matured. He could finish 500-piece puzzles by himself by the time he was four years old. He appeared to enjoy the process of recognizing patterns just as much as the outcome, which was not the result of constant repetition but rather a natural expansion of his mental faculties.

Encyclopedia of Memory

Magnus's ability to recall facts with startling accuracy was another remarkable aspect of his early intellect. By the time he was five, he knew the names, flags, and capitals of almost every nation on earth. If you asked him the name of Botswana's capital, he would say without doubt, "Gaborone." If you showed him a random flag, he would be able to identify the country and, frequently, the design's history.

There was more to this encyclopedic memory than geography. Sometimes he was so good at remembering data about vehicles, animals, and sports that grownups thought he was repeating facts. In actuality, Magnus kept his knowledge in a very well-organized manner, resembling a mental filing cabinet that he could quickly access to find the precise information he required.

Innovative Building

Magnus was gifted in both engineering instincts and creativity. He could create elaborate towns, bridges, and ships out of Lego blocks for hours on end, sometimes remembering real-world plans after only one viewing. His intricate structures and dedication to symmetry and functionality suggested a mind that actively worked to enhance patterns rather than merely absorbing them.

He would subsequently benefit greatly from this combination of memory, creativity, and spatial awareness in the game of chess, which requires the recall of thousands of positions while also requiring the quick development of novel strategy.

Pay Attention to More Than His Years

Magnus had a unique ability to focus for extended periods of time, unlike many young infants who exhibit spurts of brilliance. He was capable of completely blocking out interruptions when he was engrossed in a game, puzzle, or sketching. He was able to immerse himself in whatever activity he was working on because of this "tunnel vision," which would later prove to be one of his most useful skills at the chessboard, where concentration over long periods of time is crucial.

Even while these traits were impressive in and of themselves, his parents started to see that they were indicative of a particular type of giftedness. They were aware that Magnus's mind functioned differently than that of most kids, but they were unaware that it would show up most strongly in chess.

Initial Experiences with Chess

Magnus Carlsen's relationship with chess, like many great chess journeys, starts at home. Henrik, his father, had learnt the game as a child and played it as a recreational activity. Although he didn't play competitively, he valued the game's sophistication and intellectual challenges.

Lesson One

Henrik made the decision to introduce Magnus to chess when he was five years old, not as a structured lesson but rather as a fun experiment. He meticulously arranged the board's components in their initial locations before setting it up on the family dining table. As his father described how each piece moved pawns one or two squares forward, rooks along the files and ranks, bishops diagonally, knights in their odd L-shaped leaps Magnus listened in silence, his eyes tracking every move.

At first, Magnus appeared interested but not fixated. With his father and older sister Ellen, he played a few games, losing most of them but learning from the experience. He occasionally made rash moves or misunderstood the movement rules, like many inexperienced starters. His ability to recall the moves almost exactly and recite them to his father after every game, win or lose, set him apart from other novices.

The Inquisitive Spark

Chess started to appeal to his natural appreciation of patterns during these early games. Although the movements of the pieces were predictable, there seemed to be an infinite number of possible combinations. The board resembled an enormous riddle that could never be solved twice. This insight ignited a light within him.

He started playing more frequently after a few weeks, occasionally requesting "just one more game" from Henrik before going to bed.

Although he still made a lot of rookie errors in his early matches, his rate of growth was astounding. Magnus was already planning forward, thinking about not only his next move but the one after that, and the one after that, whereas most kids at this age play just for fun.

A Competitive Advantage Is Created

Magnus first experienced true competition in informal bouts with his sister Ellen rather than in a formal event. He was regularly beaten by Ellen, who was older, for a while. Nevertheless, Magnus viewed every defeat as a teaching opportunity rather than giving up. He started to recall the positions that had cost him the game and tried to figure out how to avoid them in subsequent contests. The defeats gradually evolved into close contests and, ultimately, victories.

A turning point was reached when Magnus realized he could win and that he could learn how to win more frequently. The delight of winning started to blend with the excitement of understanding this always shifting riddle.

Motivation Without Coercion

Henrik and Sigrun were aware of their son's increasing interest, but they took care to avoid making it into a duty. They let him play when he felt like it and take breaks when he needed to focus on other things. The game remained exciting and novel because of this independence.

They did, however, start giving him gentle prods, purchasing a better chess set, exposing him to literature for beginners, and occasionally engaging in educational games in which Henrik would describe the strengths and weaknesses of particular plays. Magnus gained a foundation from these tactful interventions without having his curiosity stifled.

The Path Ahead Starts

Magnus's unstructured play at home had changed by the time he was seven years old. In order to meet other young players and experience the excitement of competition in a social setting, he started playing chess in local clubs. He ran upon opponents who were more powerful than he was here, and the cycle of observation, adaptation, and mastery started over.

At that time, nobody could have imagined that this quiet Lommedalen youngster would grow up to be the best chess player in the world. However, many who witnessed him in those early days noticed a unique blend of dedication, creativity, memory, and focus, a

The Biography of Magnus Carlsen

combination that, in the right circumstances, might make history.

Chapter 2: Ascent in the World of Chess

Young Contests and Early Victories

Magnus Carlsen's peaceful love of chess had started to develop into something far more concentrated by the late 1990s. He had a solid foundation from his early years spent at home playing with family and reading simple novels. However, testing his skills against the larger chess community was a natural next step for any promising player.
Joining the Chess Scene in the Area
Magnus joined the Asker Chess Club, which is close to Lommedalen, when he was seven years old. For players of all ages, the club was a small but vibrant center. It was more than simply a location to play games; it was a

setting rich in experience, expertise, and most crucially for Magnus competition.

Magnus had rarely faced players that could easily defeat him since surpassing his sister in skill, but this time he did. He was not deterred by the pain of his defeats. It turned into gasoline instead. Magnus started to examine games with a childlike seriousness. Sometimes days after a defeat, he would mentally reenact the maneuvers and consider what might have been done differently.

Experience with the Tournament Early

Magnus participated in his first official youth chess event in 1999 when he was eight years old. With dozens of boards arranged in tidy rows, coffee smelling from the refreshment tables, and a calm hum of focus punctuated only by the occasional clock click, the mood was electrifying.

The Biography of Magnus Carlsen

For a novice, Magnus gave a solid performance. He impressed opponents and organizers by winning multiple matches against older and more seasoned players, even if he didn't win the tournament. People were drawn to his poise at the board, which is uncommon for a youngster. He maintained his composure despite losing, viewing every match as a teaching opportunity rather than a personal setback.

A Snatch of Triumph

In less than a year, Magnus was winning youth competitions rather than only competing in them. He won first place in his age group's Norwegian Youth Chess Championship in 2000. What was noteworthy was not just how many games he won, but also how he did it. Even at that age, he had a style that blended tactical acuity with an unexpected ability to direct games into positions that played to his strengths.

The Forms of the Competitive Mindset

Magnus's tournament strategy started to show trends that would come to define his career:

Unwavering Preparation: Prior to having a professional coach, he would read books to learn the opening lines and strive to comprehend not just the "what" but also the "why" of every move.

Psychological Resilience: He became more determined to win the next game after losing, not less confident.

He could take the initiative and attack when facing cautious opponents, or he could defend patiently against aggressive players.

Magnus was already feared on the youth circuit by the age of ten. He started receiving invitations to more competitive events as a result of his successes, where he would initially compete against adults.

Instruction and Guidance

Magnus's innate brilliance had taken him far, but many gifted young people in the chess world stagnate without the right support. His family understood that he required mentorship and disciplined training in order to realize his full potential.

The Early Role of Henrik

He was initially coached primarily by his father, Henrik. Henrik was a smart teacher who prioritized comprehension over memory, despite not being a master player. Instead of making the most obvious move, he advised Magnus to consider several options in a scenario. Magnus's approach would be based on this early reliance on independent thought.

Henrik ingrained the practice of post-game analysis. They would review Magnus's games together, move by move, following every competition or training session. The emphasis was on learning rather than condemnation, and mistakes were discussed but never in a harsh way.

Simen Agdestein's meeting

A pivotal moment occurred in 2000 when Simen Agdestein, the top chess player in Norway and a former national team football player, noticed Magnus's skill. Agdestein was well-known in the international chess world and had competed for Norway in several Chess Olympiads. Agdestein agreed to tutor Magnus through the Norwegian College of Elite Sport (NTG), where he mentored young athletes with promise, after realizing Magnus's potential.

Magnus's skill level increased significantly as a result of his training with Agdestein. He learned more complex middlegame tactics, sophisticated opening repertoires, and the value of accurate endgame play from Agdestein. Additionally, he introduced Magnus to more competitive events, occasionally setting up friendly bouts against formidable opponents.

The "Carlsen Initiative"

Agdestein and other trainers at NTG started calling Magnus's growth "The Carlsen Project." This acknowledged that they were dealing with a once-in-a-generation ability, but it wasn't an official program. In addition to honing Magnus's chess abilities, the emphasis was on developing his mental fortitude, physical endurance, and capacity to withstand the pressure of competitive games.

The Impact of Ringdal Hansen, Torbjørn

Another important person was Torbjørn Ringdal Hansen, a powerful Norwegian athlete who temporarily served as Magnus's personal trainer. By practicing specific openings, putting Magnus to the test in blitz games, and honing his tactical insight, Hansen's approach was more practical and hands-on. Magnus developed the dynamic style that would eventually make him renowned thanks to Hansen's encouragement to play aggressively when the chance presented itself.

An Increasing Reputation

By the early 2000s, Magnus was well-known outside of Norway. He started getting offers to participate in prominent youth competitions throughout Europe. He was exposed to a variety of playing styles at these tournaments, including nimble Eastern European strategists, reliable Western European positional players, and inventive attackers from various Nordic nations.

Tournament travel turned into a family activity. Henrik frequently traveled with Magnus, serving as both a parent figure and a moral compass, ensuring that the trip was interspersed with enjoyable and exploratory moments. Even though chess was becoming Magnus's life, these excursions, whether they were going to museums, touring historic cities, or sampling local cuisine, reminded him that life was more than just chess.

The New Fashion

Magnus's style started to take on its unique shape during this time of intense training and competition:

Flexibility: He felt at ease in slow, sloppy games as well as nimble tactical positions.

Confidence in Complexity: Magnus appeared to flourish in situations that were uncertain, frequently outcalculating opponents under time constraint, whilst several rookie players faltered in them.

Endgame Mastery: Coaches were impressed by his ability to play endgames with ease, extracting victories from seemingly equal positions, a talent that is uncommon in kids.

The Step Up to Mastery

Magnus was already competing at a level much beyond his age group by the time he was twelve. He quickly gained FIDE rating points and started to defeat well-established adult players. His triumphs were the result of methodical preparation, unrelenting effort, and the guidance of seasoned mentors rather than being the result of natural brilliance.

He had gone from being a promising young player to one of the world's most formidable junior players thanks to a combination of natural talent, family backing, and top-notch coaching; this trajectory would eventually catapult him to grandmaster status.

Groundbreaking Acts

Magnus Carlsen was more than simply another bright youngster by the early 2000s. Experienced players were starting to notice the outcomes he was starting to deliver. His journey was defined by these "breakthrough" performances, when talent solidified into indisputable success.

The Biography of Magnus Carlsen

Wijk aan Zee, the 2003 Corus C Tournament
At the Corus Chess Tournament in Wijk aan Zee, Netherlands, in January 2004, Magnus made his first significant international breakthrough. He was asked to perform in Group C, the third division of the esteemed competition, which often included a blend of up-and-coming artists and seasoned world masters, at the tender age of 13.

Few people outside of Norway had high expectations. After all, there were players with years of international experience, therefore the field was strong. However, Magnus shocked everyone by going undefeated in the first few rounds and defeating a number of opponents with higher ratings. His matchup with the seasoned Bulgarian Grandmaster Lubomir Ftacnik was the tournament's most well-known match.

Magnus delivered a devastating punch that startled pundits in a stunning exhibition of offensive chess, sacrificing material to tear through Ftacnik's defenses.

The triumph was so spectacular that, after studying the match, former World Champion Garry Kasparov, who was in attendance at the event, famously referred to Magnus as "a talent destined for great things." Magnus later advanced to Group B the following year after winning the Group C competition hands-down.

Grandmaster Norms's Journey

In chess, obtaining three certified "GM norms" and obtaining a rating of at least 2500 are prerequisites for becoming a Grandmaster. Magnus started gathering these standards at a startling rate for his age.

The Biography of Magnus Carlsen

First GM Norm (2004): Magnus defeated a number of formidable grandmasters to earn his first GM norm at the 6th Dubai Open Chess Championship. He wowed seasoned pros with his tactical acuity and composure under time pressure.

Second GM Norm one of the world's most difficult open events, the Moscow Aeroflot Open, is where he earned this. Magnus not only held his own but also won handily against a field full of elite general managers.

Third GM Norm: At the age of 13 years, 148 days, Magnus fulfilled all the qualifications for the Grandmaster title by completing his three norms at the 6th GM Tournament in Biel, Switzerland. This made him the third youngest general manager in history and the youngest in the world at the time.

Eliminating Well-Known Names

During this time, a blitz encounter against Garry Kasparov in 2004 stands out as one of the most remarkable events. Even though the matches were casual and quick-paced, Magnus showed glimpses of the composure and strategy that would eventually characterize his career by holding the renowned champion to a tie in one match. The young prodigy taking on the mighty monster was a momentous event.

Teachings from Losses

Not all of the events were successful. Magnus lost a few high-level competitions, including ones against formidable tactical experts who took advantage of his sporadic arrogance. However, these setbacks just helped him learn more quickly. He would thoroughly analyze these games with his instructors, pinpointing his shortcomings and modifying his preparation as necessary. Magnus's ability to quickly assimilate lessons and incorporate them into his play was one of his most impressive traits.

Acknowledgment on the International Scene

Magnus shot to international fame with a series of performances in 2003–2004. He was suddenly a worldwide chess sensation rather than merely a "Norwegian prodigy."

Media Coverage

Stories about the Lommedalen child who was beating up seasoned pros started to appear in international media and chess magazines. He appeared in articles in The New York Times, The Guardian, and Der Spiegel, frequently accompanied by pictures of his composed, nearly unimpressed demeanor at the board, which contrasted with the whirlpool of calculations going on inside his head.

As a result of admirers comparing his innate talent to the composer's effortless genius, the moniker "Mozart of Chess" started to circulate. Magnus was reticent about the title and frequently flashed a bashful smile when questioned about it.

Invitations to Prestigious Events

Opportunities came with success. Magnus started getting invited to elite closed tournaments, which are typically only open to the top 20 or 30 players in the world. These comprised:

He represented Norway's national team in the 2004 Chess Olympiad in Calvià, Spain.

He competed in the 2005 Linares Tournament, sometimes known as the "Wimbledon of Chess," against chess greats

The Biography of Magnus Carlsen

Peter Leko, Veselin Topalov, and Viswanathan Anand.

It was like being baptized by fire to face these titans. Magnus did not always win, but he showed his ability to compete at the highest level with significant draws and sporadic wins.

Taking Down the Best

Magnus defeated former World Champion Anatoly Karpov in a rapid game in the 2004 Reykjavik Rapid Tournament, one of his most well-known early triumphs on the international scene. In addition to winning, he outperformed Karpov in position and showed maturity well above his years. His status as a rising star was further cemented when he met Garry Kasparov himself later in the same event and managed a hard-fought draw.

Professional assistance and sponsorship

As fame grew, so did the chances for sponsorship. Magnus started to get funding from businesses eager to link their names to his quick ascent. This gave him and his squad the opportunity to travel more and take part in more events, exposing them to a variety of play styles.

The Change in Viewpoint

Magnus was no longer viewed as merely "promising" by the middle of the 2000s. He was thought to be a serious candidate for upcoming World Championship bouts. Prominent players started getting ready for him with the same rigor they saved for well-established grandmasters.

His versatility, in addition to his talent, was what made him unique. Depending on the opponent and position, he could alternate

The Biography of Magnus Carlsen

between sluggish positional maneuvering and aggressive tactical play. His approach blended aspects of previous champions, such as Kasparov's tenacity, Karpov's positional control, and Capablanca's simplicity, according to commentators.

The Path Ahead

Magnus's international fame marked the start of a new chapter in his journey rather than its conclusion. He had demonstrated his ability to compete with the top in the 2003–2005 tournaments. The task now was to maintain that level of performance, move up the world rankings, and eventually pursue the World Championship title.

The Norwegian boy was no longer only "one to watch" when he entered his mid-teens. The chess community was aware that he was a formidable opponent.

Chapter 3: Taking on the Role of Grandmaster

The Path to the General Manager Title

By the early 2000s, Magnus Carlsen's quick rise through the chess ranks had made it seem more inevitable than if he would ever become Grandmaster. What was really interesting was how quickly and how he would do it.

The designation of Grandmaster (GM) in the chess world is more than just a credential. The World Chess Federation (FIDE) only grants this lifetime emblem of mastery to players who fulfill two strict requirements: they must have a high rating of at least 2500 Elo and have gained three certified GM "norms" in tournaments against elite opponents. It took years for even greats like Garry Kasparov and Bobby Fischer to get there.

Magnus started climbing seriously in 2003 as his performances in international competitions started to produce results against grandmasters in addition to good results.

Initial Moves in the Direction of Norms

At the 2004 Corus C Tournament in Wijk aan Zee, Netherlands, the first significant milestone was reached. Strong International Masters and seasoned veterans were among the field's competitors, despite the tournament's formal classification as a "third-tier" group in the esteemed Corus event. With a score of 10.5/13 points, which would have been remarkable even for a fully qualified general manager, Magnus did more than just win; he demolished the competition. Organizers from all over the world took notice of this triumph and invited him to more prestigious competitions. His family and coaching staff realized that the road to the GM title was now open; all they had to do was locate events that had enough rounds to qualify for norms, enough international competitors, and fierce competition.

Dubai's First GM Norm, 2004

At the 6th Dubai Open Chess Championship in April 2004, Magnus made his first GM norm. He was up against a field full of grandmasters from all around the world at the tender age of 13 years and 3 months. Magnus played with a maturity beyond his years, guiding games into strategic confrontations rather than depending only on tactical fireworks, even in the face of the formidable opposition.

Highlights included a fine endgame victory over GM Merab Gagunashvili and a positional pressure against former World Junior Champion GM Sergey Dolmatov. Magnus reached his first GM norm with one round remaining, securing the necessary performance rating above 2600.

The Moscow Aeroflot Open: The Second GM Norm

Then, in February 2004, one of the world's most competitive open tournaments, the Aeroflot Open, took place in Moscow. Magnus demonstrated here the capacity to overcome setbacks, which is a necessary quality for any future champion.

He bounced back from a tough early loss to defeat several grandmasters in quick succession, notably GM Evgeny Alekseev. He achieved his second GM norm after his performance rating once more surpassed the norm level. Journalists covering chess started calling him "the inevitable Grandmaster."

Biel, Switzerland's Third and Final GM Norm

Magnus's last test was the Biel International Chess Festival in July 2004. He required another 2600+ performance rating to win the title because he was competing against a strong field of grandmasters. With his usual accuracy, he achieved the feat, drawing well against opponents and defeating players like GM Yannick Pelletier.

Magnus Carlsen became the youngest Grandmaster in the world and the third youngest in history on April 26, 2004, when he was just 13 years, 148 days old. His accomplishment solidified his status as Norway's first chess superstar and put him squarely on the radar of the world's best players.

Important Matches and Rivals

Even though the GM title was gained with constant performance, certain of the encounters from this era were notable for their teachings to Magnus and the chess community, as well as for their outcome.

Reykjavik Rapid. Against Garry Kasparov, 2004

There aren't many chess matches with as much symbolic significance as a youthful prodigy taking on the current king. Magnus played Garry Kasparov, who is considered by

The Biography of Magnus Carlsen

many to be the best player of all time, at the Reykjavik Rapid Tournament in March 2004. The game ended in a draw, but the process of getting there was more significant than the outcome. Magnus played without fear, maintaining a balanced stance the entire time and even applying a little pressure towards the end. Later, Kasparov acknowledged that the boy's poise under duress impressed him. Although their skills differed, they both had an unwavering competitive edge, and this match was the start of a lengthy and complicated friendship. Kasparov would later temporarily train Magnus.

Taking down Anatoly Karpov

Magnus's rapid game victory over former World Champion Anatoly Karpov in the same Reykjavik event is still regarded as one of his most well-known early triumphs.

Magnus's adaptable tactic outplayed Karpov's positional expertise in the middle game.

Magnus' triumph was noteworthy, but so was the fact that he had defeated a player who exemplified the style he was still developing. This was interpreted by many analysts as a sign of Magnus's ability to blend the finest elements of several chess traditions.

National Pride and the Norwegian Championship

Magnus's progress during these years was also significantly influenced by his participation in the Norwegian Chess Championship. Magnus viewed the tournaments as testing grounds for new openings and improving his endgame strategy because he was competing against some of his nation's best players, many of whom had decades of experience. His status as a national sports star was cemented by his triumphs in these competitions.

Norway had come together in support of their young champion by 2004. Newspapers reported on his tournaments every day, and television showed his games, giving chess a level of publicity never before seen in the nation.

Meetings with the Top Ten Players

Magnus started frequently competing against top ten players when invited to premier tournaments came in. Even though they weren't always wins, the matches against Peter Leko, Veselin Topalov, and Viswanathan Anand during this era were all masterclasses in elite chess.

Magnus witnessed personally the unrelenting aggression of a player at the top of his game against Topalov; he also understood the importance of deep opening preparation against Anand. These interactions served as stepping stones and helped him understand what it would take to dominate rather than just compete.

The Value of Misfortune

Magnus's approach to handling losses was one of the most underappreciated parts of his path to GM. In other competitions, such as Linares 2005, he lost to more seasoned, older opponents. Rather than deterring him, these losses served as motivation. Together with his trainers, he would examine them, frequently pointing out not only tactical mistakes but also more subtle psychological slip-ups, such as failing to take the initiative when it was needed or misjudging whether to press.

Magnus's rapid assimilation of these lessons allowed him to grow faster than many prodigies. His versatility and tenacity would eventually catapult him into the top echelons of the world.

Playing Style and Strategies

When Magnus Carlsen joined the Grandmaster levels in 2004, both chess enthusiasts and professional players were taking notice of his style. His strategy defied easy categorization by observers: was he a positional artist like Anatoly Karpov or a tactical genius like Mikhail Tal? In actuality, Magnus's style was developing into a distinctive blend that was based on classical ideas yet had an innately contemporary adaptability.

At the Board, a Chameleon

The Biography of Magnus Carlsen

Magnus's ability to adjust to the demands of the position, the opponent, and the tournament scenario was one of his style's distinguishing characteristics. While several grandmasters had distinct style characteristics, such as Karpov's oppressive positional restrictions, Kasparov's proactive preparation, or Fischer's unrelenting accuracy, Magnus appeared to be able to combine all of these when needed.

Magnus would lead the game into calmer waters if an opponent flourished in abrasive tactical engagements, making them demonstrate their prowess in lengthy strategic maneuvers. On the other hand, someone who felt uneasy in dynamic, open positions would push them into time difficulties, cause complications, and unleash early pawn breaks.

Some critics dubbed him "the chameleon" for his versatility, although Magnus liked to think of it as just "playing the board."

Opening Repertoire and Mental Strength

Magnus's opening repertoire in his early years was purposefully wide rather than extremely focused. He frequently steered clear of the most theoretically complex lines in favor of avoiding his opponent's preparation. He might, for instance, play the English Opening or the Accelerated Dragon instead of the ultra-theoretical Najdorf Sicilian, making his opponent think from move one instead of reciting memorized variations.

Magnus made this decision because he recognized the psychological impact of surprise, not because he lacked opening knowledge he could have prepared with the best of them. He improved the likelihood that opponents would make early mistakes by guiding them into less-analyzed territory, which provided him with advantages he could exploit with his superb middlegame and endgame abilities.

The Middlegame: Gentle Coercion

Magnus was particularly skilled at creating positions in the middlegame that seemed innocuous but held underlying tension. He frequently used nuanced tactics, moving pieces to marginally better squares and examining weaknesses without making a firm plan until the time was appropriate.

He possessed a remarkable talent for determining when an opponent's position had become unstable. His actions would then become more precise, taking advantage of little imbalances, such as a slightly weakened pawn, a mispositioned knight, or a weaker dark-square complex.

Young prodigies, who frequently used explosive techniques to win games rapidly, were not known for their patience. Magnus appeared at ease playing 60 or even 80 moves if doing so would allow him to progressively gain an advantage.

Mastery of Endgame

Magnus's skill in the endgame, which would later characterize his reign as World Champion, was arguably his most feared element. In addition to his own instinct for practical opportunities, he had studied the masterpieces of endgame play, from Capablanca to Smyslov.

Magnus managed to keep the game going even in positions that experts or engines deemed to be "equal." He would construct passing pawns, move his king into aggressive positions, and take advantage of even the smallest mistakes. Many opponents found that Magnus frequently required hours of flawless defense in a "drawn" stance, and few were able to handle the mental strain.

Compared to the Greats

Magnus's battling spirit was frequently compared to Kasparov's, his endgame persistence to Fischer's, and his positional awareness to Karpov's by analysts. Although nice, these comparisons did not fully convey the situation. Magnus was combining the best elements of several legends and adding his own contemporary twist, not copying any one of them.

Magnus worked in a computer-aided age where adaptability and rapid change were critical, whereas past champions planned for particular lines and themes. His approach demonstrated a thorough comprehension of both opponent psychology and chess positions.

Overcoming Obstacles

Magnus Carlsen faced challenges on his path to becoming a complete player despite his extraordinary talent and quick ascent. These difficulties, which ranged from general failures to psychological and personal trials, helped him develop into the tough competitor he would become.

Dealing with the Elite: Initial Setbacks
Magnus faced players in the world's top 10 with decades of expertise at the highest level after he started competing in super-tournaments. Some of the losses were heartbreaking, but others were unavoidable.

For instance, Magnus lost badly to Veselin Topalov, who was at the top of his game at the time, in Linares 2005. Magnus's position was completely destroyed by Topalov's aggressive tactics, and the game ended in less than thirty moves. This served as a sobering warning to a young player used to dominating that at the highest level, talent alone would not be enough.

Such losses did not depress Magnus; rather, they served as a diagnostic tool. Together with trainers, he would thoroughly examine them, examining both tactical errors and more serious strategic blunders. This self-examination practice eventually turned into one of his strongest traits.

The Weight of Expectations

Magnus was already being heralded in the press as a potential world champion by the time he was in his midteens. Invitations to renowned events and sponsorship opportunities were brought about by the publicity, but it also put a great deal of strain on them. Every draw with a lower-ranked opponent was questioned, and every loss was examined.

Here, Magnus's family was very important. His parents encouraged him to pursue hobbies, travel, and socialize with people in order to prevent chess from taking over his entire personality. He was able to escape burnout, which had destroyed previous rising stars, because of this equilibrium.

Getting Used to Various Time Controls

A rising focus on quicker time limits, blitz and rapid games that demanded snap decisions without compromising quality also accompanied Magnus's early career. Magnus understood that he needed to adjust, even if his natural style valued strategic maneuvering and thorough thought.

He started preparing especially for these formats, honing his rapid assessment techniques and understanding when to trust his gut feeling over laborious computation. He would become one of the world's most feared quick and blitz players as a result of his versatility.

How to Handle Tournament Fatigue

Back-to-back matches against the world's best players are common in elite tournaments, with little downtime in between. This could be mentally taxing for a teenager.

Magnus initially had trouble controlling his energy, occasionally getting off to a strong start but losing steam as the game progressed.

He eventually established dietary, sleeping, and mental-resetting habits. He would go for walks, listen to music, or even play light sports to decompress in between bouts.

Handling Streaks: Positive and Negative

Magnus had both winning streaks and slumps, just like every other player. The difficulty was in maintaining emotional stability in the face of recent outcomes. Overconfidence could result from a run of wins, while self-belief could be damaged by a run of defeats.

Magnus discovered that every game should be approached as a stand-alone task, free from the weight of past results. Resilience is just as crucial in world championship matches as preparation, therefore this mental discipline would be quite helpful.

Prodigy to Professional Transition

Making the transition from "the talented kid who can beat grandmasters" to a reliable, elite professional was arguably the most difficult task of all. This required not only honing technical abilities but also embracing the arduous process of preparation, which included spending hours learning endgame subtleties, analyzing opening novelties, and staying up to date with the quickly changing chess engine landscape.

By the conclusion of this time, Magnus had not only conquered these obstacles but also used many of them to his advantage. His psychological fortitude, adaptability, and unwavering work ethic had now caught up to his natural brilliance. His next big step forward competing for the top slots in the world rankings was set in motion.

Chapter 4: Champion of World Chess

The Championship Journey

Even though it seemed that way to onlookers, Magnus Carlsen's ascent to the World Chess Championship stage was not an overnight occurrence. Many in the chess community conjectured that he would eventually contend for the game's most coveted title as soon as he was 13 years old and received his Grandmaster title. However, the nearly ten-year journey to that point was replete with consistent advancement, calculated professional decisions, and a purposeful development of his chess mindset.

Moving Up the Rating Scale

Magnus's rating increased steadily in the years after he was named GM, demonstrating both his innate talent and his desire to get better. For someone still in his teens, he accomplished a tremendous feat by breaking into the world's top 10 by 2008.

This climb was remarkable not only because of the sheer number of jumps but also because of how they were accomplished. Magnus wasn't cherry-picking events to boost his ranking or focusing on a certain tournament format. He was competing against, and frequently beating, elite players in blitz, fast, and traditional formats. Even though he had not yet participated in a World Championship match, his ability to consistently defeat top-tier opponents had earned him the top spot in the FIDE rankings by 2010.

Rejecting the Candidates Cycle of 2011

Magnus made one of the most unexpected choices of his career in 2010 when he decided not to compete in the 2011 Candidates Tournament, which was the official competition to choose the world title challenger.

He felt that the format, which featured short matches and specific tie-break methods, did not represent the ideal means to identify a challenger. His rationale was unconventional but insightful. Critics said this was a hazardous move that would postpone his hopes of winning a title. But Magnus thought that since he was young and his form was becoming better, there would be other chances and when he did run for the title, he would do so on terms that prioritized a real test of chess prowess over tricks.

Super-Tournaments Dominance

Magnus demonstrated that his confidence was well-founded during the course of the following two years. Almost every super-tournament he participated in, including the London Chess Classic, Tal Memorial, Bilbao Masters, and Wijk aan Zee, saw him win or place strongly.

In addition to boosting his spirits, these wins demonstrated to his prospective rivals that he could maintain a high level of performance in a variety of forms, competitive settings, and continents. Magnus was establishing a reputation as the young man who could defeat anybody, anyplace, in any kind of game.

London's 2013 Candidates Tournament

In 2013, Magnus made the decision that it was time to challenge for the world championship. Eight of the top players in the world competed in the double round-robin Candidates Tournament that year in London.

Vladimir Kramnik, a former World Champion renowned for his meticulous preparation and positional expertise, was his principal opponent in the field. Carlsen and Kramnik soon found themselves in a heated two-horse contest.

Magnus played well in the first half of the competition, but his anxieties started to show in the second half. The race was thrown wide open when he lost to Vassily Ivanchuk in the penultimate round. Magnus and Kramnik were deadlocked going into the final round, but Carlsen prevailed on tiebreaks. Magnus won the tournament by his better tiebreak score after both players lost their most recent matches Kramnik to Ivanchuk and Carlsen to Peter Svidler.

Magnus subsequently said he was as relieved as he was excited by the dramatic, nerve-racking conclusion. Because of the victory, he was eligible to face the current champion, Viswanathan Anand, later that year.

Overcoming Anand Viswanathan

There was a generational clash during the 2013 World Chess Championship match. Five-time World Champion Viswanathan Anand, who was admired for his quick thinking and decades of top-tier expertise, was on one side. Magnus Carlsen, a 22-year-old Norwegian prodigy who had never played a match before but had a history of defeating the best in the world in tournament play, was on the opposing side.

Setting the Scene: India's Chennai

The champion had a home-court advantage because the tournament was played in Chennai, India, Anand's hometown. With press conferences, live commentary, and thousands of supporters eager to watch to see if their idol could defeat the youthful challenger, the Hyatt Regency Hotel turned into a center of chess activity.

Along with his father, Henrik Carlsen, his longtime second, Jon Ludvig Hammer, and a small but close-knit support group, Magnus arrived in Chennai. As the reigning champion, Anand enjoyed the support of a whole country and a greater entourage.

Feeling Each Other Out in the First Rounds
Neither player took too many chances, and the first two games ended in draws. Carlsen's plan was obvious: guide the game into middlegame and endgame situations, steer clear of highly theoretical opening skirmishes, and test Anand's defensive strategy over an extended period of time.

The Biography of Magnus Carlsen

Magnus was playing "Magnus chess," according to observers, which involves avoiding needless complications and maintaining a balanced situation with a few modest edges that he could attempt to convert. Anand, on the other hand, was focusing on his strong points, which are rapid tactical perception and thorough preparation.

Game 5: Breaking the Deadlock

Game 5 was the pivotal moment. In a rook endgame that appeared to be equal, Magnus started to exert light pressure by moving his king and rook to make Anand's position vulnerable. At first, most observers predicted that the game would end in a draw, but Magnus persisted, and it paid off. Magnus jumped in and turned the lead into a full point when Anand made a small mistake.

Carlsen's triumph was classic: there were no fireworks or clear-cut knockouts, just constant pressure until the opponent gave up.

Game 6: Consecutive Victories

Game 6 was the follow-up punch if Game 5 was a body blow. Once more, Magnus successfully negotiated a challenging middlegame to reach an endgame where he had a little but persistent advantage. This time, Carlsen won for the second time in a row after Anand's resistance gave up earlier. The trend had clearly shifted in favor of the young Norwegian, who now led 4–2 in the 12-game encounter.

Changes in Psychology

The atmosphere in Chennai changed after Game 6. Normally composed, Anand appeared to be under more obvious stress. Magnus, on the other hand, seemed at ease;

he smiled during news conferences after games and entered the playing hall with his usual easy assurance.

Carlsen's group understood that it was important to avoid complacency. With decades of victories in a variety of settings, Anand was a master of comebacks. Magnus kept playing sensibly, taking measured chances but never engaging in careless gambling.

Game 9: The Final Outcome

Magnus only needed one more point to secure the title with the score at 5-3. Playing Black in Game 9, he maintained a tight but balanced position and held Anand to a draw. He now had 6½ points, which is sufficient to win without having to play the final three games.

The Start of a New Era

Carlsen became the 16th undisputed World Chess Champion and the second-youngest in history after Garry Kasparov as soon as the draw was decided. He had ushered forth a new era in chess at the age of 22, overthrowing a living icon in Anand.

After-Match Responses

Magnus's endurance and skill to take advantage of even the tiniest opportunities were commended by Anand, who was gracious in defeat. Anand remarked, "He has a great talent for keeping the pressure on and avoiding mistakes."

As usual, Magnus presented the win as merely another career milestone and minimized it as a personal victory. He said, "I'm thrilled to have won, and I'll do everything in my power to defend the title."

The Biography of Magnus Carlsen

The victory prompted a national celebration in Norway. Magnus came home to a hero's welcome, complete with parades and formal celebrations, after television networks paused their usual programming to show the match's closing seconds.

Effect on the World of Chess

Carlsen's triumph marked a sea change for the sport as well as a personal achievement. A new generation of players were influenced by his style, which prioritized psychological fortitude and practical play over profound opening theory. Because of his youthfulness and charm, he also garnered corporate sponsorships and media attention, which helped chess become more widely discussed than it had been for decades.

Even though Magnus' rule was only getting started, he had already changed the definition of what it meant to be a 21st-century World Chess Champion.

Rivalries and Title Defenses

Winning the World Chess Championship is a huge accomplishment, but maintaining it is frequently far more difficult. There have been chess champions throughout history who reigned supreme for a short time before losing to the following generation of opponents. The years that followed Magnus Carlsen's triumph over Viswanathan Anand in 2013 were a test of his endurance, flexibility, and mental toughness in addition to his skill.

During Carlsen's stint as champion, chess players were becoming more skilled and ready to challenge him after years of studying his games. Nevertheless, Magnus managed to control the match in each championship defense, frequently combining deft strategic maneuvering with unwavering poise under duress.

The Rematch with Anand in 2014

After winning the 2014 Candidates Tournament in Khanty-Mansiysk, Russia, a year after their initial match, Anand was granted the opportunity to face Carlsen once more. The rematch was scheduled for Sochi, Russia, in November.

Anand was more prepared this time and resolved to avoid making the same mistakes as Chennai. He took the advantage in the second game after striking first and catching Carlsen in a quick tactical move. Magnus falling behind in a World Championship match was an uncommon sight.

However, the way that champions handle hardship is frequently what defines them. In Game 3, Carlsen responded right away with a positional masterwork to tie the score. Then came one of Carlsen's most well-known games, Game 6, in which he pressed in a somewhat better position until Anand made a mistake under time pressure, which many commentators believed to be the match's psychological turning point.

In the end, Magnus prevailed 6½–4½, effectively retaining his title for the first time. It was a message to the chess community that overthrowing him would require more than just better preparation; it would require weeks of unwavering anxiety.

The Karjakin Test in 2016

The challenger was Russia's Sergey Karjakin, who won the Moscow Candidates

Tournament in 2016. The encounter in New York City turned out to be one of the most intense of Carlsen's career, and Karjakin was dubbed the "Minister of Defense" for his extraordinary fortitude in trying circumstances.

Karjakin effectively thwarted Carlsen's attempts to generate winning opportunities for the whole of the match. Following a rare instance of the champion going overboard, Karjakin shocked the chess community by defeating Carlsen in Game 8. Carlsen appeared truly scared for the first time in his title defenses; he even skipped the press conference after the match, which resulted in a fine from FIDE.

However, Carlsen leveled the score in Game 10 with a clean positional win, just when it appeared that things might be about to change. Rapid tiebreaks were used to decide the title after 12 traditional games ended 6–6. Here, Carlsen's dominance under quicker time controls was evident as he prevailed 9–7 overall after winning two games and drawing the others.

The match's last move, a masterful queen sacrifice that resulted in a checkmate, was immediately recorded in chess history as the ideal fusion of strategy and flair.

The Caruana Standoff in 2018

After a strong showing at the Berlin Candidates Tournament, Carlsen's opponent in 2018 was the American Grandmaster Fabiano Caruana. The peculiar reason the London match was historic was that all 12 of the classical games ended in draws.

The games themselves were complicated, despite the scoreline suggesting a lackluster event. In multiple matches, Caruana tested Carlsen to the limit, and many commentators believed the challenger had lost legitimate opportunities to win.

Rapid tiebreaks, Carlsen's preferred method, were used to end the match once more. Magnus swept the tiebreaks 3–0 in a dominating performance, firmly holding onto his crown. There was no dispute over who was the superior quick player, but his success rekindled discussions over whether the championship system should prioritize classical games more.

The Nepomniachtchi Collapse in 2021

The COVID-19 epidemic interrupted the 2020 Candidates Tournament, which ended in 2021 with Ian Nepomniachtchi as Carlsen's opponent. Both players exchanged draws in the opening rounds of the match in Dubai, which started out evenly.

However, everything changed in Game 6. Carlsen won a grueling endgame that broke the deadlock in what turned out to be the longest game in World Championship history, spanning 136 moves and almost 8 hours. Nepomniachtchi never bounced back; he committed a number of uncommon errors in the games that followed, and Carlsen easily won 7½–3½.

It would be Carlsen's final title match performance, but it was also one of his most dominant.

2022: Leaving the Title Behind

Citing a lack of desire, Carlsen surprised the chess community in 2022 by declaring he would not defend his championship against the next Candidates Tournament winner.

The Biography of Magnus Carlsen

After almost ten years in the top spot, he declared that his attention would turn to other objectives, such as online competitions, quick and blitz chess, and personal endeavors.

Others viewed it as a sign of Carlsen's confidence he had nothing more to prove in the traditional World Championship cycle while others saw it as an abdication. Additionally, his choice was a reflection of a larger reality: Carlsen had already solidified his reputation, and the game of chess was more important than the championship itself.

Effect on the Community of Chess Players

Magnus Carlsen's impact on the chess community goes well beyond his performance. Carlsen's rule has been as much about cultural influence as it has been about competitive domination, from changing the way the public views the game to encouraging a spike in young players' engagement.

Increasing the Media Presence of Chess

Chess had long been seen as a specialized sport prior to Carlsen's ascent, with sporadic spikes in popularity during world championship matches. That dynamic was altered by Carlsen.

He was a natural media icon because of his young charm, attractive appearance, and approachable manner. He participated in celebrity events, modeled for fashion brands such as G-Star RAW, and had appearances in advertisements. These endeavors enhanced rather than diminished his competitive image, elevating chess to a level of popularity not seen in decades.

The Boom in Online Chess

In adopting internet chess, Carlsen was a trailblazer. Long before online competitions were popular, he often took part in them. The Magnus Carlsen Chess Tour is a series of elite internet events with fast and blitz time constraints and top-notch commentary that Carlsen started after the COVID-19 epidemic in 2020 stopped over-the-board chess.

Both experienced players and casual fans who valued the quicker tempo and easily accessible streaming formats were drawn to these events, which drew enormous viewership. Record numbers of people signed up, according to websites like Lichess and Chess.com. This increase is frequently ascribed to Carlsen's prominence and the ease of access to online competition.

Motivating the Upcoming Generation

The generation of fresh talent that Carlsen sparked is arguably his greatest enduring impact. Carlsen has been publicly cited as an inspiration by athletes from Uzbekistan, India, the United States, and other countries. His approach, which emphasizes practical decision-making above memorized openings, appeals to those who wish to build a well-rounded game.

Several grandmasters have emerged in nations like India, which have experienced a chess revival. Many of these individuals grew up watching Carlsen's matches versus Anand and other players. Carlsen's matches were shown live on national television, which helped chess become a popular sport in Norway.

Modifying the Game of Chess

The strategic orientation of elite chess was also impacted by Carlsen's supremacy. He questioned the conventional wisdom that a match without an early advantage was bound to end in a draw by emphasizing the importance of grinding out victories from equal positions.

Top players adjusted, enhancing their psychological stamina and ultimate strategy. Often attributed to the "Carlsen Effect," tournament preparation started to move away from merely memorizing opening moves and toward a more comprehensive grasp of every aspect of the game.

A World Ambassador for the Game

Carlsen has accepted the role of ambassador, whether it is through chess promotion in schools, exhibition matches versus amateurs, or amusing social media banter. In addition to using his position to promote humanitarian causes, he co-founded Play Magnus, an organization dedicated to chess instruction and promotion.

More than any other player since Garry Kasparov, he has arguably contributed to the worldwide spread of chess by bridging the gap between elite competition and grassroots engagement.

Community Legacy

Carlsen is still the world's top-ranked player and a regular at elite tournaments after giving up the traditional crown. His influence on the chess community will last for generations thanks to his unique combination of media acumen, accessibility, and competitive excellence.

Magnus Carlsen has, in many respects, changed the definition of a chess champion. Nowadays, winning titles isn't the only goal; you also need to inspire millions of people, change the game's culture, and leave the board in a better state than when you started.

Chapter 5: Beyond Chess, Life

Magnus Carlsen's reputation as the "Mozart of Chess", an unmatched strategist, a fierce rival, and a world champion who broke records is deeply ingrained in the public consciousness. However, to view him solely through the prism of 64 squares is to overlook a more comprehensive image. Carlsen is not a reclusive chess enthusiast who dedicates all of his free time to learning opening lines. He has pursued a variety of hobbies, had an active lifestyle, and developed a public character that unites popular culture and sport outside of the competitive sphere.

This chapter examines that aspect of him, how his interests, passions, and forays outside of the chessboard have influenced not just his character but also his impact on a worldwide scale.

Hobbies and Interests

Although Carlsen's thoughts frequently go different paths, his life outside of chess is not an escape from introspection. He has pursued a range of interests that enhance his competitive career, from pop culture and music to sports and travel.

Passion for Athletics

Football, or soccer, is maybe Carlsen's biggest pastime if chess is his career obsession. He is a passionate fan of Real Madrid, a Spanish football team renowned for its legendary lineups and lengthy history. His dedication goes much beyond simple fandom; he argues tactical decisions, keeps a careful eye on match statistics, and has even competed in fantasy football competitions with the same competitive fervor as his chess aspirations.

Out of almost seven million participants, Carlsen briefly topped the Fantasy Premier League global rankings in 2019, making headlines. It demonstrated his analytical thinking, meticulousness, and early trend recognition. He echoed the statistical mentality that guides both football and chess strategy when he stated, "It's all about expected value and probabilities."

Carlsen also likes to play football for fun. His participation in local matches with friends, journalists, and other professionals during tournaments contributes to his physical conditioning, something many people don't identify with chess players. In between competitive rounds, he frequently participates in spontaneous games in parks or sports centers.

In addition to football, he has expressed interest in basketball, tennis, skiing, and hiking sports that let him connect with Norway's natural environment and provide a break from the long hours of focused indoor competition.

Love of strategy games and puzzles

Perhaps it should come as no surprise that a chess genius likes other games that require pattern recognition and logic. Carlsen enjoys playing crosswords, Sudoku, and quiz contests. He frequently has an advantage in these kinds of activities due to his quick recall and lateral thinking; in fact, he has even been known to outscore more experienced players in trivia games.

He has also studied poker as a means of comprehending various types of strategic interaction, rather than as a career. There are fascinating similarities between the psychological aspects of competitive chess and the risk management and psychology of bluffing in poker.

Exploration and Cultural Interest

Carlsen has visited nearly every continent as part of his tournament calendar, but for him, travel involves more than merely switching between competitions. He schedules time to explore the towns he travels to, whether it is by trying the local food, going to museums, or strolling around neighborhoods to get a sense of daily life.

He has stated that he particularly enjoys Mediterranean and Asian cuisine, and he frequently looks for tiny, genuine eateries rather than popular tourist destinations. He embraced the local cuisine while in India for his world championship matches versus Anand, albeit he acknowledged altering the level of heat to his Norwegian taste.

Carlsen has developed informal cross-cultural networks and friendships via his travels, which has given him a cosmopolitan perspective uncommon among professional athletes.

Personal Style and Fashion

Carlsen has a distinct sense of personal style even though he is not fashion-obsessed. His partnership with the Dutch designer apparel brand G-Star RAW was a significant step in fusing fashion and sport. By posing with supermodels in photo shoots and advertising campaigns, Carlsen contributed to dispelling the myth that chess players lack style or are socially awkward.

Carlsen frequently chooses to wear sharp casual attire or fitted blazers even in tournament situations, giving off an air of professionalism while remaining approachable. His clothing selections quietly support his brand as a contemporary cultural icon and champion.

Media Consumption and Reading

Carlsen's reading preferences are varied, in contrast to the cliché of the chess prodigy buried in opening theory books. His interests in behavioral psychology, history, and biographies frequently touch on his comprehension of human decision-making.

He also watches popular entertainment. He has talked about how he likes to watch famous TV shows, such as comedies and high-budget dramas, as a method to decompress and escape the stress of competition.

Playfulness and Humor

One aspect of Carlsen's public presence is his sardonic, frequently caustic sense of humor. He has employed humor as a social tool and a means of humanizing his image, whether it is through humorous remarks on social media, playful trolling of opponents in online blitz games, or mocking himself in interviews.

This creativity has also been shown in over-the-board situations: he occasionally selects purposefully odd openings in simultaneous demonstrations against amateurs, pushing himself to win from less accustomed positions. Fans are reminded by these instances that Carlsen still views chess as a game to be played rather than just a profession to be managed.

Media Presences and Support

Magnus Carlsen is well-known outside of the chess community. He has used his position to establish himself as a well-known public personality in a variety of media during the last ten years. High-profile interviews, magazine pieces, TV cameos, and advertising campaigns are just a few of his appearances.
Movies and Television
Carlsen frequently combines lighthearted entertainment with subtly promoting chess in his TV appearances. He has been on several chat shows in Europe, "The Colbert Report" in the United States, and sports broadcasts where he offers commentary on football games. Through these performances, chess

has been made accessible to audiences that might not have otherwise played the game.

He had a brief appearance on the Norwegian television series Skavlan in 2016, where he engaged in light conversation and showed how to plan ahead, not just in chess but also in life. Additionally, he has made appearances in chess documentaries, such as Magnus (2016), which provides viewers with an inside look into his journey from boyhood to world champion.

Partnerships with Brands and Advertising

The combination of Carlsen's youthful appeal, academic credentials, and widespread international reputation makes him marketable. He has endorsed international businesses such as Nordic Semiconductor, Kindred Group, Simonsen Vogt Wiig (a

Norwegian legal company), and G-Star RAW.

He is a global ambassador for Unibet, one of his most prominent collaborations. His interest in probability and prediction is evident in this partnership, which fits in well with his analytical abilities. Initiatives to encourage responsible gaming are also part of the cooperation; Carlsen has openly endorsed this cause.

Tech and Chess Collaborations

Carlsen has taken the initiative to integrate technology and chess. He was a co-founder of Play Magnus, a business that uses tournaments, learning resources, and apps to make chess accessible to players of all ability levels. Since then, Play Magnus Group has grown by purchasing additional chess-related websites. In 2022, it merged with Chess.com,

The Biography of Magnus Carlsen

solidifying Carlsen's position as a major player in the online chess community.

Carlsen has been the face and the impetus behind initiatives to update chess's online presence through these endeavors. In contrast to certain previous generations of athletes who opposed technological integration, he is open to embracing new platforms.

Photographs and Features in Magazines

Prominent magazines like Time, The New York Times, Der Spiegel, and The Guardian have included Carlsen's story. These characteristics frequently draw attention to his dual persona as a young guy with a wide range of interests and as an outstanding competitor.

He has been able to portray an image that is both elegant and approachable through photo sessions for lifestyle magazines, sports periodicals, and fashion labels. By portraying chess as a lively, young activity, these pictures aid in dispelling outdated preconceptions.

Panels and Public Speaking

Carlsen has attended conferences, sports summits, and educational events, but he is not a self-promoting celebrity in the conventional sense. He has discussed the value of critical thinking, self-control, and flexibility under duress skills that are applicable to many aspects of life outside of chess.

These interactions have established him as a thought leader in strategic thinking and cognitive performance in addition to being a sporting hero.

Presence on Social Media

The Biography of Magnus Carlsen

Carlsen keeps up-to-date accounts on social media sites like Facebook, Instagram, and Twitter. His posts cover anything from football commentary to funny memes and tournament information. This relaxed, intimate style enables him to engage with supporters on a human level, demonstrating that even the greatest chess player in the world likes to talk about the game from last night or post a photo from a trip.

His Twitch streaming and involvement in events such as Chess.com's Titled Tuesday have helped increase the appeal of chess among younger, tech-savvy audiences during online tournaments.

Entering the Pop Culture

Carlsen is the most well-known living representative of chess in a time when the game has regained popularity due in part to

The Queen's Gambit. His impact has extended to video games, as seen by his participation in commercial partnerships and chess-themed apps.

He also contributed his image to Fantasy Chess, a lighthearted variation that blends competitive chess predictions with aspects of internet fantasy sports.

Juggling a Career in Chess with Media Work
The ability to balance media and commercial commitments without sacrificing his competitive advantage has been one of Carlsen's strongest suits. Even while traveling for commercial work, Carlsen has continued to prepare for tournaments and maintain strict training regimens, in contrast to some athletes who become sidetracked by their celebrity.

The Biography of Magnus Carlsen

He ensures that media opportunities are consistent with his brand identity and beliefs by treating them as a component of his professional portfolio. Carlsen maintains his authenticity whether recording an ad, conducting an interview, or promoting an event online; this trait appeals to both advertisers and fans.

Magnus Carlsen has greatly increased his influence outside of the chessboard by leading a rich personal life, engaging in a variety of pastimes, and keeping up a strong media presence. He has shown that a world champion may be an interesting cultural figure in addition to being a highly analytical athlete. By doing this, he has introduced chess into areas that it has not previously occupied, guaranteeing that the game reaches new audiences and encouraging the next generation to view chess as a method of thinking, living, and interacting with the world rather than merely a hobby.

Entrepreneurship

Although Magnus Carlsen's brilliance is most apparent on the chessboard, his vision is widely applicable in the business sector. Carlsen has embraced the role of an entrepreneur, in contrast to many previous chess champions who concentrated almost entirely on competition. His endeavors encompass everything from internet platforms and app creation to collaborations that integrate chess with technology, education, and entertainment.

Making chess more approachable, interesting, and visible in the contemporary world has been the explicit goal of Carlsen's business endeavors. He has used his international profile to start businesses, make investments in creative concepts, and work with digital companies always keeping growth and sustainability in mind.

Play Magnus Group

The Play Magnus Group (PMG), established in 2013, has been the focal point of Carlsen's business endeavors. The original concept was surprisingly straightforward: develop an application that lets users compete against a digital representation of Magnus Carlsen at various ages, ranging from 5 to his current skill level.

In addition to offering a distinctive and customized training experience, the app was a great combination of novelty and educational tool, allowing fans to experience what it was like to confront the prodigy at different points in his career. However, Carlsen and his group didn't end there. Play Magnus developed into a multi-pronged chess business that offers a range of digital goods and services.

PMG grew over time by purchasing or joining forces with a number of well-known chess companies, such as:

Chessable is an educational platform that caters to both novices and experts, with an emphasis on spaced repetition and interactive courses.

New in Chess is a prominent producer of educational books and chess magazines.

iChess is a library of online video tutorials.

Carlsen contributed to the development of a centralized ecosystem where players could interact with the chess community, play, and learn by combining multiple platforms under one roof.

The world's biggest online chess site, Chess.com, combined with the Play Magnus Group in 2022. With Carlsen at the core of its power, this combination produced a single, dominant force in online chess.

Technology in Education and Chess

Chessable stands out among the PMG purchases as a game that has the potential to revolutionize education. Carlsen's own conviction in purposeful practice aligned with Chessable's science education methodology, which is founded on the idea of spaced repetition. Through courses that he co-created or approved, the platform gave him the opportunity to directly share his knowledge with a large online audience.

Carlsen worked with others on a thematic learning series that addressed endgames, middlegame tactics, and openings. Because of his ability to clarify difficult concepts, these courses were beneficial to students of all skill levels, and his name on them ensured considerable visibility.

Strategic Alliances and Sponsorship

As part of his business philosophy, Carlsen aligns himself with companies that share his interests and principles. He has collaborated with businesses in technology, gaming, and finance in addition to fashion brands like G-Star RAW. His partnership with Unibet serves as an excellent illustration of how to use his reputation for analysis to responsibly and data-drivenly promote sports betting.

He has experience with Nordic Semiconductor, Kindred Group, and the online trading platform Skilling. In each instance, Carlsen's endorsements are not just motivated by profit; rather, they support his overarching goal of encouraging creativity, smart risk management, and critical thinking.

Creation of Online Tournaments

Carlsen was quick to change course when the COVID-19 outbreak disturbed over-the-board chess in 2020. He started the online super-tournament series known as the Magnus Carlsen Chess Tour, which brings together the top players in the world. With expert commentary and creative formats that kept spectators interested, the events were transmitted live throughout the world.

Among the tour's highlights were:

Invitational to Magnus Carlsen

Masters of Chess

Examining Open

Masters of Airthings

These competitions showed that elite chess may flourish online without sacrificing its competitiveness. Sponsors and viewers who might not have otherwise participated in digital chess were drawn in by Carlsen's strong brand.

Cross-Industry Engagement and Esports

Carlsen has demonstrated a strong interest in esport, seeing similarities between chess and competitive gaming. He has appeared as a guest at esport competitions, collaborated on streaming projects, and talked about how the two worlds are comparable in terms of psychology, training, and audience interaction.

Carlsen has introduced chess to younger audiences that are used to live streaming, quick commentary, and engaging fan interaction by tying the game into esports culture.

Individual Investments

Carlsen has alluded to investments in Internet businesses, especially those that are centered on gaming, artificial intelligence, and education, even if he keeps much of his personal financial decisions confidential. His long-term goal seems to be to provide viable ways for chess to continue to be relevant in a world that is becoming more and more digital.

Philosophy of Business

Carlsen's strategy for business is similar to his strategy for chess: strategic risk-taking, flexibility, and an unwavering quest for positional advantage. He is a unique example of a sports champion who is also a skilled entrepreneur because of his willingness to try out new forms, accept unusual alliances, and adjust to shifting market conditions.

Contribution to the Popularization of Chess

Carlsen has had a significant influence on chess's appeal. Even though chess has a long history of notable winners, like José Raúl Capablanca, Bobby Fischer, Garry Kasparov, and Viswanathan Anand, no one has done so more than Carlsen to popularize the game in the twenty-first century.

Dispelling the Chess Player Stereotype

Prior to Carlsen's ascent, a chess player was frequently portrayed in popular culture as an eccentric recluse who was out of touch with society and socially uncomfortable. Carlsen's youthful, athletic, fashionable, and media-savvy public persona contributed to the deconstruction of that impression.

He demonstrated that being a chess champion could be aspirational in ways other than cerebral prowess by making appearances in fashion ads, sporting events, and entertainment media.

The Digital Age of Chess

Carlsen has played a key role in bringing chess into the modern digital age. Top-tier chess is now more accessible than ever thanks to his online competitions, involvement in streaming events, and active participation on websites like Twitch and YouTube.

In order to improve the game's viewership, he has been open to experimenting with additional time controls, like quick and blitz forms. Hundreds of thousands of people watch his online bouts live, which is comparable to the attendance at big esports events.

Motivating the Next Generation

Carlsen has been able to engage youthful viewers thanks to his approachable demeanor and sympathetic humor. Through online platforms, he frequently interacts directly with fans, occasionally streaming his thoughts during games or playing casual games versus amateurs.

Aspiring chess players now look up to him as an example of how perseverance, curiosity, and hard effort can lead to success without compromising one's uniqueness.

The "Carlsen Effect" in the Development of Chess

Global chess activity has significantly increased during the time of Carlsen's dominance:

During his world championship reign, online platforms have recorded spikes in the number of sign-ups and games played.

Courses featuring or supported by Carlsen have seen record enrollment on chessable and other learning sites.

Once confined to specialized periodicals, media coverage of chess has now spread to popular sports and lifestyle outlets.

A significant contributing factor to this rise has been Carlsen's continuous reign as world champion, even if other factors like the pandemic-driven surge and the success of The Queen's Gambit have also played a role.

The Gambit Connection of the Queen

The Biography of Magnus Carlsen

Chess experienced an unheard-of spike in popularity in 2020 following the release of The Queen's Gambit on Netflix. Carlsen welcomed the trend by taking part in media debates, offering commentary on how chess was portrayed in the series, and utilizing the occasion to highlight internet chess resources.

His readiness to serve as the game's public face during this boom assisted in directing the renewed enthusiasm into long-term participation rather than a fleeting trend.

Outreach Education

Carlsen has backed efforts to teach chess in schools, both domestically and abroad. These programs encourage youngsters to play chess as a way to improve their patience, critical thinking, and problem-solving abilities.

His participation has contributed to the validity and funding of these programs, and his own narrative is a powerful illustration of the positive effects of early chess exposure.

Crossover Appeal and Celebrity Matches

Actors, musicians, and athletes are among the personalities Carlsen has faced in exhibition matches. These events are frequently shown as special features or streamed online, drawing viewers who may not have been particularly interested in chess before.

Carlsen has broadened the cultural reach of chess by extending its reach into other entertainment domains.

Durable Legacy

Carlsen will always be remembered for his contributions to chess's popularity, regardless of whether he wins the title of world champion. Being a worldwide ambassador, digital inventor, and cultural icon, he has completely reinvented what it means to be a modern chess champion.

His contributions to the development of Play Magnus Group, online competitions, and teaching materials will continue to influence chess for many years to come.

The Hero Outside the Board

Magnus Carlsen's impact goes far beyond his actions during world championship contests. His economic endeavors have changed the chess industry, and his public presence has introduced the game to audiences it had previously been excluded from.

Carlsen has transformed chess into a more dynamic, visible, and culturally relevant sport by combining business innovation, media presence, and competitive prowess. He has demonstrated that the game's future

The Biography of Magnus Carlsen

depends on seizing fresh chances for development and interaction in addition to upholding existing customs.

Chapter 6: History and Prospects

The narrative surrounding Magnus Carlsen's time at the top of chess is already well established. However, Carlsen's impact is being acknowledged immediately, in contrast to many others whose contributions are only fully recognized after their careers are over. His unique combination of competitive superiority, contemporary business acumen, and cultural significance has already changed the course of chess in the twenty-first century.

This chapter looks at his broader contributions to the game as well as his developing role as a mentor and inspiration to the upcoming generation of players.

Inputs into the Game

Beyond his individual matches and tournament triumphs, Carlsen has made significant contributions to the game of chess. He has expanded the sport's fan base, changed the chess economy, and reinvented playing styles. His strategy has been both revolutionary bringing chess into the digital era in ways no other world champion has tried at this scale and evolutionary building on the work of previous champions.

Changing the Way You Play

Magnus Carlsen's style of play has been described as "universal," indicating that he can play almost any position with ease. Carlsen thrives on adding complexity to seemingly straightforward positions, in contrast to players who mostly rely on memorized opening theory or astute tactical gambits.

His ability to extract victories from positions that seem drawn is one of his defining characteristics. Anatoly Karpov and José Raúl Capablanca have been compared to this "endgame grind," but Carlsen has elevated it to a new level. By doing this, he has encouraged a new generation of players to place more importance on skill, perseverance, and mental pressure than on opening preparation alone.

His versatility is demonstrated by his success in blitz, quick, and classical time controls. A more comprehensive understanding of what it means to be a complete chess player in the current era has been facilitated by this adaptability.

Increasing Access to Elite Chess for All

The Biography of Magnus Carlsen

The majority of world-class chess matches were invitation-only, closed events with little live broadcast and significant barriers to entry for amateur fans before Carlsen's ascent to prominence and his online initiatives.

Millions of people around the world were able to watch elite chess thanks to Carlsen's advocacy for internet super-tournaments during the pandemic that were aired with live commentary and interactive features. He disrupted the traditional division between the professional and amateur domains by doing this.

Thanks to his guidance, fans can now watch, learn, and even play against simulations of the world's top players on websites like Chess24, Chess.com, and the Play Magnus app. The way that audiences view chess has been irrevocably changed by this change.

Making Chess Commercial Without Undermining Its Integrity

It has always been difficult to make money off of chess while also honoring its intellectual value. Carlsen's leadership in starting and expanding the Play Magnus Group and then combining it with Chess.com showed that chess could be made profitable while still meeting the demands of dedicated players.

Players, commentators, and organizers now have additional sources of revenue thanks to the professionalization of online chess tournaments with appropriate sponsorships, prize money, and production quality. Aspiring professionals now have more employment options thanks to this, which is probably going to be a long-lasting aspect of Carlsen's legacy.

Popularizing Chess in Culture

Carlsen has demonstrated that chess can survive outside of its conventional bounds by participating in fashion campaigns and working with well-known companies. Chess has been repositioned as a contemporary, approachable, and even aspirational activity because of his involvement in events involving athletes, celebrities, and esports leaders.

In addition to attracting casual followers, this cultural shift has increased chess's attractiveness to sponsors, expanding the game's opportunities for players of all skill levels.

Increasing the Preparation Standard

Even though Carlsen is well-known for prioritizing flexibility over extensive, limited opening preparation, his training schedule is nonetheless quite demanding. His emphasis on mental toughness, psychological readiness, and physical fitness has impacted how other elite athletes practice.

Elite athletes now frequently include sports psychology, diet planning, and gym sessions in their regimen habits that Carlsen helped popularize. The takeaway is unmistakable: mastering movements alone is no longer enough to be a great chess player in the current era.

Initiating the World Chess Boom

Carlsen's contribution to the chess boom of the 2010s and 2020s cannot be overstated. Although epidemic lockdowns and The Queen's Gambit had an impact, Carlsen's ongoing supremacy, online accessibility, and openness to public interaction have been crucial in maintaining this rise.

The surge in young people joining chess clubs, the growth of online competitions, and the expanded coverage of chess in the mainstream media are all examples of the "Carlsen effect." Under his leadership, the game has evolved from a specialized intellectual activity to a more popular competitive sport.

Maintaining Traditional Chess While Adopting New Formats

Some were concerned that classical chess would be threatened by the popularity of quick and blitz forms. The coexistence of all three time constraints has been guaranteed by Carlsen's well-rounded strategy. He has demonstrated that chess can flourish in a variety of formats without losing its core qualities by being exceptionally good at each.

In addition to making faster forms more commercially and viewer-friendly, his influence has helped maintain the status of the traditional World Chess Championship.

An Outlook on Chess's Future

It has been implied by Carlsen that his ultimate objective is to leave chess in a better state than when he started. His emphasis on accessibility, education, and top-notch events implies that his legacy will include both his individual accomplishments and the game's structural advancements.

The Inspirational and Mentoring Role

Beyond his own achievements, Carlsen's impact on upcoming players is already influencing his legacy. Carlsen has influenced a generation to rethink what is possible in chess, either directly through mentoring or indirectly through his example.

Direct Coaching and Mentoring

Carlsen has worked with talented young players in casual settings despite not having a conventional teaching academy. He has made educational content available to many players worldwide through online sites such as Chessable and Chess24, which effectively serve as mentorship.

Carlsen has also provided one-on-one coaching to identify up-and-coming players, offering insights into attitude, preparation, and the pressures of professional chess. His method, which is characteristic of his own manner, focuses more on encouraging autonomous thought than it does on providing rigorous technical training.

Providing a Professional Example

Carlsen provides young chess players with an example of professionalism that goes beyond the board. His focus on physical fitness, mental toughness, and personal branding has demonstrated that chess success may be based on a variety of factors.

In a time when chess players are becoming more well-known, juggling competition with media commitments and business prospects, this example is particularly helpful.

Breaking Down Geographic Representation Barriers

Players from areas that have not previously had representation at the highest level have been motivated by Carlsen's ascent from Norway, a nation with no established chess traditions. He has demonstrated that anyone, anywhere in the world, can reach the top with the correct mix of skill, perseverance, and encouragement.

This has a special effect on young chess players in South America, Africa, and Southeast Asia, where the sport is expanding quickly but infrastructure is still lacking.

Motivation Through Play Style

Numerous players have been motivated by Carlsen's approach to prioritize flexibility, originality, and in-depth knowledge over rote memorization. Younger generations have been inspired to embrace perseverance and resourcefulness by his ability to transform humble positions into wins.

In their interviews, many young players point to Carlsen as both their chess hero and an example of how to behave under pressure.

Promoting Sportsmanship and Fair Play

Carlsen has been outspoken about upholding chess's integrity, especially in the digital age when computer-assisted cheating is becoming a bigger problem. He has reaffirmed the significance of fairness as an unavoidable component of competitiveness by adopting moral positions, even when they are divisive.

Younger players traversing the emotional highs and lows of competitive chess might learn from his emphasis on respect for opponents, humility in success, and serenity in failure.

Having Direct Conversations with Learners and Fans

Carlsen engages with chess players of all skill levels via social media, internet streaming, and open Q&A sessions. A top player's life is demythologized and made more relatable through these exchanges. This accessibility is very inspiring for young players since it demonstrates that even the world's finest players belong to the same community.

Building Up the Talent of Tomorrow

Young players benefit much from the competitions and platforms Carlsen has created, especially during the pandemic. In particular, competitions like the Julius Baer Generation Cup pit top veterans against up-and-coming talent, providing the latter with crucial exposure against top-tier opponents. Carlsen has made sure that his mentoring goes beyond one-on-one interactions and provides systematic support for talent development by institutionalizing these chances.

The Ripple Effect Over Time

The ramifications of Carlsen's mentorship and motivation are probably going to last for decades. Whether they become pros, instructors, or community chess ambassadors, players who grew up watching his games and learning from his platforms will take those teachings into their own careers.

In this way, the flourishing community of players and followers he leaves behind can be used to gauge his genuine legacy in addition to trophies and rating points.

A legacy in motion

The legacy of Magnus Carlsen is a dynamic and ever-changing phenomena. His innovations in tournament design, commercialization, cultural outreach, and playing style have already changed the game in ways that will last for many generations.

The Biography of Magnus Carlsen

His function as an inspiration and mentor guarantees that the upcoming generation of chess players will uphold his principles of professionalism, ethics, and flexibility in addition to his technical teachings.

Although it is impossible to foresee exactly where chess will be in 20 or 30 years, it is obvious that Carlsen's influence will be clearly seen in the direction it takes.

Accomplishments and Honors

The pinnacle of a career for the majority of chess players would be a single world championship or a brief period at the top of the ratings list. Such achievements, in Magnus Carlsen's opinion, are merely pieces of a much bigger picture, a career characterized by constant innovation, unwavering greatness, and an almost uninterrupted supremacy that has lasted for well over 10 years. His accomplishments, both on and off the board, are astounding in both quantity and diversity, encompassing both cultural recognition and competitive victories.

Titles of World Chess Championships

Magnus Carlsen has the record for one of the longest and most prosperous reigns as World Chess Champion. In 2013, he won the title by defeating Viswanathan Anand in Chennai, India. He then successfully defended it against Anand again in 2014, Sergey Karjakin in 2016, Fabiano Caruana in 2018, and Ian Nepomniachtchi in 2021.

This streak is noteworthy not only for the quantity of titles he earned but also for the range of methods he used to hold onto them. In traditional games, Carlsen defeated Anand handily in 2014. He had to rally from a deficit against Karjakin in 2016 before winning the match in quick tiebreaks. Before Carlsen won the quick playoffs in 2018, all of the traditional matches against Caruana ended in a tie, which had never happened in championship history. His triumph over Nepomniachtchi in 2021 was among the most lopsided in the history of the modern championship.

Carlsen showed not only competence but also remarkable adaptability by holding onto his title despite changing formats, new competitors, and changing chess theory.

FIDE World Championships for Blitz and Rapid

In 2014 and 2019, Carlsen became the first person to hold simultaneous titles in blitz, fast, and traditional chess. This "triple crown" is particularly uncommon since it necessitates proficiency with a wide range of time controls:

Classical games include a strong emphasis on psychological stamina, strategic preparation, and thorough calculation.

Accuracy must be maintained while making decisions more quickly in rapid chess.

The main components of blitz are speed, intuition, and steely nerves.

It takes a balance of traits that are uncommon in a single player to excel in all three. What it means to be a "complete" chess champion has been redefined by Carlsen's supremacy in all formats.

Records and Peak Ratings

The highest-ever FIDE rating of 2882 was attained by Carlsen in May 2014. His record-breaking run of more than ten years at or near the top of the ratings list is even more astonishing.

With 125 games from 2018 to 2020, Carlsen also holds the record for the longest winning streak in top-tier classical chess. This run of wins and draws against almost every elite player in the world demonstrated not only his tenacity but also his steady competitive advantage.

Prominent Tournament Wins

Even while world titles take center stage, Carlsen has amassed an impressive record of victories in tournaments:

Carlsen has defeated elite fields year after year in the Wijk aan Zee/Tata Steel Chess Tournament, winning it a record eight times as of 2023.

The Sinquefield Cup is one of the most prominent competitions outside of the world championship cycle, featuring numerous wins over loaded squads.

Events on the Grand Chess Tour: Consistent success in blitz, combination, and quick forms.

He has a level of mental tenacity and motivation that few champions have equaled, as seen by his ability to perform at his best during major events and in regular circuit play.

Olympiads and Team Contests

Carlsen has participated in several Chess Olympiads on behalf of Norway, frequently guiding the squad to victory over nations with much more illustrious chess histories. Even though Norway hasn't won a gold medal yet, Carlsen's presence has given the national team a dignity and competitiveness that was previously unthinkable.

The Biography of Magnus Carlsen

Honors Other Than Competitive Chess
Beyond the chessboard, Carlsen's accomplishments have been acknowledged:
Norwegian Sportsman of the Year: Having won numerous titles in his native nation, he is comparable to Norway's most renowned athletes in other sports.
Nominee for the Laureus World Sports Award: Chess players rarely receive recognition on a worldwide athletic platform.
Time 100 Nominee: Being mentioned in discussions about the most significant individuals in the world.
These accolades highlight his influence in chess as well as in other cultural and athletic contexts.
Achievements in Digital and Cultural Impact
Carlsen contributed to the creation of one of the most resilient online chess ecosystems in

history with the Play Magnus Group and the subsequent merger with Chess.com. Since these initiatives have expanded accessibility, given players new sources of income, and drawn in millions of new fans, their success is in and of itself a triumph.

Carlsen has become an advocate for the game in ways that few past champions have ever tried thanks to his appearances in popular culture, which range from late-night chat programs to fashion ads.

A Career in the Hall of Fame While Still Active

The fact that Carlsen completed all of his accomplishments while still in his prime may be the most remarkable feature of his list. Carlsen continues to be a dominant force in every format he joins, in contrast to previous winners who began to lose their edge in their

30s. This implies that his record book is still open.

Looking Ahead

At this point in Magnus Carlsen's career, the question of "what's next?" is just as fascinating as "what has been?" Even though Carlsen has already accomplished every possible milestone in competitive chess, his goals and the larger shifts in the chess community indicate that his impact will only increase in new and changing ways.

Leaving the Classical World Championship Behind

Citing a lack of interest in the conventional format, Carlsen declared in 2022 that he would not be defending his classical world title in the 2023 cycle. The chess community

The Biography of Magnus Carlsen

was taken aback by this choice, but it also suggested that his priorities had changed.

Instead of announcing his retirement, Carlsen has prioritized online competitions, blitz and quick formats, and fresh competitive challenges. This change could eventually increase chess's appeal to audiences in the modern era who are used to faster-paced models.

Remaining the Best-Rated Player in the World

Carlsen has remained the world's top-rated player despite not holding the title of formal world champion. Because of his continued involvement in top tournaments, he continues to be a key player in competitive chess and a standard by which up-and-coming players can be judged.

Encouraging Online Chess as a Popular Activity

Carlsen has stated unequivocally that online chess is a permanent feature of the game's future rather than only a pandemic-era occurrence. He still supports and takes part in top-notch online competitions with expert production values, commentary, and worldwide accessibility.

This approach is consistent with esport and other sports developments, where audience growth depends heavily on digital involvement.

Developing the Upcoming Generation

Carlsen has alluded to a rising desire to coach up-and-coming players, either through official programs or by organizing competitions that highlight up-and-coming athletes. This emphasis on intergenerational rivalry is shown in his participation in competitions such as the Julius Baer Generation Cup.

Potential Diversification of Careers

Even if chess is still the major focus, Carlsen has shown interest in extracurricular pursuits including poker, business endeavors, and even fantasy sports. His desire to compete implies that he will attack any such endeavors with the same ferocity that has characterized his chess career.

The Long Term: Establishing a Durable Infrastructure for Chess

Carlsen's outlook for the future probably calls for him to keep influencing the chess industry's commercial and cultural landscape. This could entail building platforms that combine competition, instruction, and entertainment, increasing educational outreach, and further integrating chess into schools.

Individual Objectives and Difficulties

Although Carlsen's public remarks imply that he is happy with his professional path, it can be difficult for someone who has accomplished everything to find fresh inspiration. It remains to be seen if that results from off-the-board projects, new formats, or personal rating aspirations.

Conjecture Regarding Retirement Schedule

Carlsen has not provided a specific timeframe for leaving the professional chess scene. He might continue to compete at a high level for many more years because of his mental toughness and physical fitness. His readiness to abandon the traditional title, however, demonstrates that he prioritizes his own happiness over custom.

A Legacy in Motion

In the future, Carlsen's impact is probably going to show up in three primary ways:

1. As a player, keep raising the bar for competition.
2. As a Business Leader: Establishing enduring chess businesses.
3. As an Ambassador: Maintaining the relevance of chess in international society.

Whatever the details, the upcoming years should be just as significant if not as foreseeable as his years of dominating championships.

Printed in Dunstable, United Kingdom